Introducing
BEETHOVEN

ROLAND VERNON

Chelsea House Publishers
Philadelphia

First published in hardback edition in 2001
by Chelsea House Publishers, a subsidiary of
Haights Cross Communications. All rights reserved.
Printed and bound in China.

First published in the UK in 1994 by
Belitha Press Limited, London House,
Great Eastern Wharf, Parkgate Road,
London SW11 4NQ, England

Text copyright © Roland Vernon 1994
Illustrators copyright © Ian Andrew 1994

Editor: Robert Snedden
Designer: Andrew Oliver
Picture Researcher: Vanessa Oliver

3 5 7 9 8 6 4

The Chelsea House World Wide Web address is
http://www.chelseahouse.com

Library of Congress Cataloging-in-Publication Data applied for.

ISBN: 0-7910-6038-1

Picture acknowledgments:
AKG, Berlin: 6 top, 6/7, 7 top, 9 top & bottom, 10, 11, 12,13,14,16 top,
17, 19 middle, 20 bottom, 21 bottom, 22 top, 23, 24 top right, 25, 26, 28, 29
Bridgeman Art Library: 6 bottom, 19 top, 22/23, 245 top left
E.T. Archive: back cover right, title page, 8, 16 bottom, 18, 21 top
Mary Evans Picture Library: back cover left, 7 bottom, 20 top
Mansell Collection: 19 bottom
Popperfoto: Cover, 9 middle, 24 bottom

CONTENTS

INTRODUCING BEETHOVEN

LUDWIG VAN BEETHOVEN was born at a time of great change in Europe. It was an exciting time, when people were attempting to break free from past **oppression**, and scientific discoveries promised a whole new way of life for ordinary men and women. Encouraged by these changes, artists, writers, and musicians also began to introduce fresh ideas into their work, and a great era in the history of art came into being—the era of the **Romantics**. Beethoven lived in the heart of this turbulent Europe. He was not just carried along by the changes going on around him, but actually brought some of them about. He was a revolutionary and a musical genius; after Beethoven, music would never be the same again.

Fig. 255.—Beethoven on his Death-bed.
(From a Drawing by Danhauser.)

A NEW WORLD IS BORN

George Washington (1732–99), hero of the American Revolutionary War, became the country's first president.

*T*he progressive thinkers and writers of the late eighteenth century, such as Jean Jacques Rousseau and Thomas Paine, wanted to see a world in which everyone would be equal and free. However, this meant bringing down the existing rulers by force. The 1770s saw a bitter war for independence in America, and 1789 witnessed the bloodiest uprising of them all—the **French Revolution**.

Coalbrookdale, beside the Severn River in Shropshire, became one of the world's first industrial centers.

Around this time scientists and engineers were inventing new machinery that would change people's lives in a different way. This non-violent revolution had effects that were as far-reaching as any brought about by war. The **Industrial Revolution**, as it became known, saw the beginnings of heavy industry and the decline of village and country life as people moved to the towns to take jobs in the new factories and mills. One of the most important engineers of the time was **James Watt**, whose work on steam engines between 1776 and 1781 soon led to the birth of the railways.

Painters and poets reflected the mood of the age. In Germany the poet **Schiller** expressed his hatred of tyranny, while in England **William Blake** lamented the miserable working conditions of the poor. Artists also started to look toward landscape for their inspiration. **Caspar David Friedrich**, a German painter, and **William Wordsworth**, an English poet, both demonstrated in their work this fascination with the power of nature. In such an age of unrest and upheaval, heroes are born, particularly military and political heroes, such as Napoleon. It was a time

Many writers, thinkers, and painters felt that the French Revolution meant the beginning of a new age of hope.

"The Traveler Above the Mist," by Caspar David Friedrich (1774–1840), shows a popular image of a lonely walker contemplating the mystery of nature.

when people were admired for their new ideas, and for having the courage to stand by them. This brought about great reforms for ordinary people, but it also brought about a fashion for artists to cut themselves off from the world and brood over their own thoughts.

REVOLUTIONARY THINKERS

The English-born writer Thomas Paine (1737–1809) did more than simply write about revolution; he took an active part in the American Revolutionary War, distributing leaflets to Washington's troops and raising money for supplies. After returning to England, he published *The Rights of Man* (1791–2) in support of the French Revolution, which made him very unpopular. He believed that monarchies should be abolished in favor of republics. He was influenced by the writings of Jean Jacques Rousseau (1712–78), a French thinker, whose book *The Social Contract* (1762) begins with the words, "Man is born free, and everywhere he is in chains." His works about nature, religion, and education were also influential in the Romantic Movement.

A MUSICAL CHILD AT THE COURT

The Archduke Maximilian (Elector of Cologne) arriving at his palace. Maximilian was a brother of the Hapsburg Emperor.

*I*n the eighteenth century people often became professional musicians because it was the family trade, just like a baker or a cobbler. The skills of the craft were passed on from father to son, and beyond. There are many examples of great composers who belonged to musical families, for example, Mozart, **Bach** and **Purcell**. Ludwig van Beethoven was another.

At the time of Beethoven's birth in 1770, musicians depended for their income on rich **aristocrats** and rulers. They would try to become members of the palace court, composing and performing in their **patron**'s private chapel, theater, or drawing-room. The Beethoven family was employed at the court of the Elector of Cologne, who was the ruler in Bonn, Germany.

Like his father before him, Beethoven was brought up surrounded by the musicians and the music of the Elector's court.

Beethoven's grandfather, who was also called Ludwig, was the first of the family to work for the Elector. He started as a bass singer, and eventually rose to be **Kapellmeister**, the most senior musician at the Elector's court. His son, Johann, was also a singer in the chapel, and gave lessons on the piano and violin.

The Elector of Cologne's palace in Bonn, Germany.

Left, Johann van Beethoven and far left, Maria Magdalena van Beethoven.

In 1767, Johann married Maria Magdalena, a twenty-year-old widow, and the couple went on to have seven children. Only three of them survived infancy, all boys, the eldest of whom they called Ludwig.

Mozart, the child genius, at the harpsichord while his sister Nannerl sings, and his father, Leopold, plays the violin.

From an early age Ludwig showed that he had a rare musical gift, and his father encouraged him to work hard at practicing both the piano and violin. Perhaps he was hoping young Ludwig would cause a similar sensation as the child Mozart, who had just ten years before toured the courts of Europe, performing with his father and sister. At one concert that Ludwig gave, he was announced as being six, although he was actually seven, so that the audience would be even more impressed with his skills.

Johann was perhaps a little too strict, and it is said that Ludwig did not have a very happy childhood. Matters got even worse when his father began to drink.

$\mathcal{A}$
CLASSICAL
TRAINING

Christian Gottlob Neefe, who became Court Organist at Bonn in 1782, was Beethoven's teacher and senior colleague.

hen Ludwig was about eight years old, he began to take lessons from another musician at the court, **C.G. Neefe**. He soon became Neefe's assistant as court organist, and at the age of eleven even directed the Elector's theater orchestra when his teacher was away on other business. It was thanks to Neefe that Beethoven learned the **classical** rules of composition and mastered his technique as a **keyboard** player. Before long he was earning his own salary at the court and was composing some short piano pieces, which he dedicated to the Elector.

Neefe decided that his young student should be given the opportunity to travel, and in 1787 the Elector gave his permission for Ludwig to visit Vienna, the Empire's capital. It is likely that on this trip Ludwig met and had some lessons with Mozart himself. As Beethoven played the piano, Mozart is said to have remarked, "Keep your eyes on him; some day he will give the world something to talk about."

MOZART, THE YOUNG GENIUS

Wolfgang Amadeus Mozart (1756–91) is considered by many to be the most gifted musical genius that ever lived. He discovered very early on that he could compose music with little difficulty. He was bursting with musical ideas and would work out a whole piece in his head before writing it down. He was a complete master of all musical forms, including symphonies, concertos, sonatas, and operas, and he composed a huge number of works. Some other composers were jealous of his extraordinary gifts, and much of his short life was spent struggling for recognition. Haydn was a good friend, however, and the two composers learned a great deal from each other.

The four-year-old Mozart can be seen here among the musicians at the wedding of the Emperor Joseph II.

Mozart and Beethoven together in 1787. Mozart's early death in 1791 prevented a second meeting between the two great composers.

The exciting experience of Vienna was cut short after only two weeks, when Ludwig heard from Bonn that his mother was dying of **tuberculosis**. He returned to a depressing life at home—his mother and baby sister died, his father drank more heavily, and the household fell into disorder. Nonetheless, Ludwig was beginning to make his name as a fine musician, and he gained the support of several wealthy friends, such as **Count Waldstein**.

The famous composer Joseph Haydn passed through Bonn in 1790 on his way to London and again on his return in 1792. He was introduced to the court's budding genius. Once he had seen Beethoven's compositions, he was convinced that the Elector should be persuaded to allow Ludwig leave from the court once more. This time he would go to Vienna as Haydn's personal pupil.

Vienna, at the center of the Austrian Empire and Europe as a whole, had a great musical history. Beethoven's arrival there was to mark the beginning of a new chapter for music in the city.

HAYDN

Joseph Haydn (1732–1809) linked two musical generations. He developed the composing methods of people like Bach and Handel and paved the way for the revolutionary experiments of Beethoven. Haydn understood the way an orchestra works very well and worked hard to get the best possible effect from it. He wrote 106 symphonies, and his writing for orchestra was an important influence on both Mozart and, later, Beethoven. Haydn spent most of his life as court composer for the Esterházy family, but his fame spread throughout Europe. He was always a favorite in Vienna and was welcomed with great enthusiasm when he visited England. His kindness earned him the nickname "Papa."

The year 1792 marked the beginning of a long war between France and an alliance of European countries. On September 20, 1792, the French successfully forced back their enemies at Valmy.

VIENNA, THE HEART OF AN EMPIRE

Marie Antoinette, wife of Louis XVI and Queen of France, was the sister of Austria's Emperor, Joseph II.

he road along which Beethoven traveled to Vienna was no longer as safe as it had been on his first visit. In 1792, the effects of the French Revolution could be felt right across Europe. It all began on July 14, 1789, when the people of Paris rose up in arms against their rulers. King Louis XVI was deposed in 1792, and the French **Republic** proclaimed. Other European countries, including Austria, took sides with the imprisoned king and declared war on France. Convoys of troops and supplies now marched to the battlefront. Just two years after Beethoven left, Bonn was invaded by the French. The Elector escaped, never to return.

Vienna was the capital of the Austrian Empire, and home of the Imperial family, the Hapsburgs. The Hapsburg court had a great reputation for encouraging the arts and had made Vienna the most important musical center of Europe. Aside from the royal circle, several other wealthy families in the city spent money supporting musicians, which meant there was more chance of success for a struggling young composer in Vienna than anywhere else in the Empire.

The Hapsburg family surrounded by their court at a grand concert in Vienna.

Composers such as Mozart and Haydn had written music that was popular with ordinary citizens, and people began to flock to public concerts. The great composers could at last be heard and appreciated by many, not just a privileged few. When Beethoven arrived in Vienna, composers were beginning to be thought of less as servants to the rich, and more as special people in their own right.

In 1793, King Louis XVI of France and his wife, Marie Antoinette (who was an Austrian Hapsburg), were publicly beheaded by the revolutionaries in Paris. The Royal families of Europe shuddered with fear.

THE VIRTUOSO

Antonio Salieri (1750–1825) was a popular composer and director of music at the imperial court in Vienna for 36 years. Beethoven was his pupil and dedicated three violin sonatas to him.

Haydn was by now in his sixties and much loved in Vienna as a composer. But Beethoven was not happy with him as a teacher, and it was not long before he began to look elsewhere for lessons. He was impatient to start experimenting with his music. He found Haydn too old-fashioned, too keen on "rules" of composition, and also a little careless in his correcting. Without letting Haydn know, he turned instead to three other teachers: Schenk, Albrechtsberger, and Salieri, the court conductor.

Although he was still being paid by the Elector in Bonn, Beethoven now had to find employment in Vienna. His father had died, so he had to send money back home to his two younger brothers. As a pupil of Haydn, he was introduced to several fashionable Viennese aristocrats, many of whom already knew of him through his friendship with Count Waldstein, and he began to make a name for himself playing the piano at private parties. He would **improvise**, making up the music as he went along, in a style that was different from anything his audiences had heard before. He would get carried away in a stormy

passion, smashing his hands against the keys, and sometimes breaking piano strings. He wanted to do more than entertain people; he wanted to thrill them.

Beethoven made his reputation as the most exciting keyboard player in Vienna just at the time when the piano was beginning to replace the **harpsichord**. The piano was much more suited to Beethoven's style of performance—it allowed for loud or soft playing, which was impossible on the harpsichord.

Beethoven also proved himself as a concert pianist, sometimes playing his own music, sometimes other people's. He was given much support by Prince Lichnowsky, a musical aristocrat, who had once studied with Mozart. It was to this man that the young composer dedicated several of his early compositions, including the famous *Pathétique* **Sonata** for the piano.

HARPSICHORDS AND PIANOS

The harpsichord is a type of keyboard instrument that was first developed in the fifteenth century. The strings inside it are plucked by leather or quill **plectra** when the keys are struck, and the player cannot vary the sound very much. Harpsichords were made bigger and bigger in order to increase their volume for solo playing, and they became very expensive to build. The piano, first invented in Florence around 1700, has little padded hammers inside that strike the strings. The harder the keys are struck the harder the hammers hit the strings and the louder the sound that is made. Pianos were cheaper to make than harpsichords and allowed a musician to express more feeling. They were considered to be much more suitable for the style of music being written at the time, and within about fifty years harpsichords had been completely replaced by pianos as instruments for performance.

The pianos of Beethoven's day were nothing like as loud or strong as modern versions and could barely stand up to his exciting new style of playing. The wealthy people of Vienna were dazzled by the wild young virtuoso, and he soon became very popular.

15

THE NIGHTMARE BEGINS

At the age of thirty, Beethoven was well-known as a pianist, conductor, and composer of exciting new music. But it was at this time that he also became aware of a frightening problem that was going to change his life forever. He was going deaf. He had first begun to worry about the condition as early as 1798, but over the next three years, his hearing had grown steadily worse. None of the treatments he tried were successful.

Deafness was hard for Beethoven to accept. His successful career as a pianist, conductor, and teacher became more and more difficult as his hearing grew worse. Eventually he would have to give up performing and teaching altogether. He felt lonely, frightened, and worried about how he would support himself.

The village of Heiligenstadt nestled into the hills outside Vienna, with the Danube River in the distance. Heiligenstadt has since been swallowed up into the city.

A portrait of Beethoven, aged thirty-three.

He began to avoid meeting people, partly because he was embarrassed about his deafness and wanted to keep it a secret. He imagined enemies who would try to ruin his career if they knew. In 1802, he wrote a letter to his brothers. For some reason he never sent it, and it was found among his papers after his death. The letter has become known as the Heiligenstadt Testament, after the village of Heiligenstadt (just north of Vienna) where he wrote it. In the letter Beethoven describes his depression and even talks of suicide. But he also writes that he has accepted his fate and is resolved to continue, despite his deafness.

Part of the Heiligenstadt Testament. Although he admits to despair, Beethoven realized he still had much work to accomplish.

One important result of his sad condition is that he was forced into spending more time alone, composing. A good musician does not need to hear sounds in order to compose, but can imagine them from the written notes on the page. Beethoven struggled on alone, and as he did so, his music began to change. It was as if his deafness had opened the door to a new musical language.

EROICA

NAPOLEON AND THE REVOLUTION

Napoleon Bonaparte was born on the island of Corsica in 1769. He went to a military school in France and showed great promise in the army. He was promoted to brigadier general at the age of 24 after successfully dealing with an uprising in the French port of Toulon. Two years later he was put in command of the French army in Italy and won spectacular victories against Austria. He fought the British in Egypt, where his fleet was destroyed by Admiral Nelson, and he returned to France to plan his rise to political power. By this time he was a national hero, and in November 1799, he took the title of First Consul, becoming the most powerful man in France. Napoleon seemed to be the man who had saved the Republic and kept the revolution alive, but he soon became a **dictator**. In 1804 he strengthened his position by having himself crowned Emperor of France. This was seen by many as a betrayal of the revolution.

The revolutionary painter Jacques-Louis David shows Napoleon crossing the Alps on his way to victory. He is deliberately made to look heroic, and is often compared to Hannibal of ancient times.

The more Beethoven shut himself off from everyday life in Vienna, the more he turned in on his own feelings. His music became longer, deeper, and darker, as Beethoven searched further and further into himself. It developed on a lonely path, with less and less regard for past traditions.

One of the ideas he explored at this time was his belief in freedom for all people. Although he had been brought up in an aristocratic court, and had delighted the rich people of Vienna with his playing, Beethoven thought it very unfair that just a few noble families should have so much power and privilege, while most people remained poor. In a way, he shared the hopes of the revolutionaries in France. It just so happened that one particular revolutionary had recently risen to great fame and had become for many people the hero of the moment—Napoleon Bonaparte.

It was with Napoleon in mind that Beethoven began to compose what was to be his own favorite work, his Third **Symphony**, known as the *Eroica* ("Heroic"). It was different from anything ever written before and is thought by many to mark a turning point in musical history. The *Eroica* lasts twice as long as a typical symphony by Mozart or Haydn. It is a fierce work that contains some ear-splitting clashes and sweeps the listener along on a wave of powerful feeling. Beethoven is arguing a point with this music, not just entertaining his listeners.

When Napoleon crowned himself Emperor of France in 1804, Beethoven was so disappointed he tore the dedication "Bonaparte" off his music. Napoleon had become what Beethoven most hated—another tyrant.

Beethoven continued to expand his musical ideas with the **quartets** he wrote for the Russian **ambassador**, Count Razumovsky, in 1806. Once again he was cutting new ground. The four musicians at first found the music so difficult to understand, they thought Beethoven was having a joke at their expense.

David's grand painting of Napoleon's coronation, in 1804. Behind the Emperor sits Pope Pius VII.

The first edition, eventually dedicated to Prince Lobkowitz.

The original manuscript has the "Bonaparte" dedication scratched out.

FIDELIO

Beethoven wrote only one **opera**, *Fidelio*, and it caused him a good deal of trouble. In fact, he called it his "crown of martyrdom," because it took him so long to get right.

Beethoven had once before begun work on an opera but did not get very far. He composed slowly at the best of times, but writing for the theater was altogether a new challenge for him, and he soon got bogged down. It was not until he came across a story line that really excited him that he felt ready to try again.

The story he found came originally from a true account of something that happened during the French Revolution. A man is unjustly imprisoned for his beliefs and is only saved from a terrible death by the action of his devoted wife. She disguises herself as a man and rescues him at gunpoint from his would-be murderer.

It was the perfect theme for Beethoven, who, as we have seen, had strong feelings about the importance of freedom and justice. On a deeper level, he felt that he himself was like the prisoner in the story—condemned to a life of miserable loneliness in the dungeon of deafness.

The dramatic climax of *Fidelio*. The scene is being used in this picture to advertise food products.

THE PRISONERS' CHORUS

One of the most moving moments in *Fidelio* comes in the first act when the prisoners are allowed up from their dungeons to breathe fresh air and see the daylight for a short time. The prisoners represent all people who are victims of injustice. These are innocent men, unfairly condemned, but in this magical scene they rise up to the light, united in happiness, hope, and song. It is this revolutionary theme in the opera that Beethoven found so exciting—the gift of freedom to people who have spent their lives in oppression. Stage directors have found different ways over the years of expressing the important message of this scene. Here is an example of the 1935 production in Berlin—ironically, staged when Hitler was in power.

In November 1805, just before *Fidelio*'s first performance, the French army invaded Vienna. Beethoven's friends and supporters fled the city, and the opening night was attended for the most part by Napoleon's officers. The opera at this stage was under-rehearsed and also far too long. It flopped after only three performances. Beethoven changed it a little and tried again in 1806, but this time he quarreled with the theater manager and had it closed after two performances. A third version, with a new **overture**, new spoken **dialogue**, and many changes to the music, was put on in 1814. This time it was successful, and ever since it has been a favorite all over the world.

The French army parading in front of Vienna's royal palace after their conquest of the city.

One of Napoleon's greatest victories was against the Austrians at the Battle of Ulm, fought in September and October 1805. Vienna fell shortly afterward.

A RESTLESS MAN

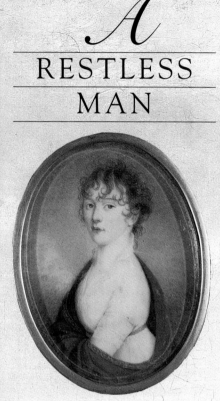

Above, Countess Giulietta Guicciardi, a pupil of Beethoven, to whom he dedicated the *Moonlight* Sonata. She was one of his greatest loves, and her marriage to Count Gallenberg in 1803 came as a shock to the composer.

Above right, Beethoven spent long, lonely hours in his study, struggling with musical ideas.

*B*eethoven worked very hard between the years 1806 and 1812; many of his most famous masterpieces date from this time, such as his Violin **Concerto**, his fifth and sixth symphonies, and the *Emperor* Concerto. But during these important years, the composer was far from content. He was suspicious of everyone, bad-tempered, and stubborn. Unfortunately, his loyal friends were the first to suffer, and he ended up quarreling with many of them. He poured scorn on fellow musicians who performed his works, and his treatment of household servants was nothing short of cruel. He was rude in public, scruffily dressed, and disorganized. In fact, he felt so restless and uncomfortable, he did not even keep the same home for more than a few months at a time. Although he would have liked a wife, and fell in love several times, he never managed to find a woman who was prepared to share this sort of life.

The agony of deafness only made matters worse and left him feeling lonelier than ever. There was also the problem of money. He gave an enormous concert of his new works in 1808, but the program was far too long for most people's liking, and his piano-playing suffered because of his poor hearing. It was not a very successful evening. The question had to be faced—how was he to earn a living? He nearly accepted a job as senior court musician to the King of Westphalia, Jérôme Bonaparte (Napoleon's brother). But three aristocrats combined resources and offered him a salary for life, just if he would remain in Vienna. He accepted, and stayed where he was.

When life in the city got too much for him, Beethoven would find comfort in the countryside; and as he walked, deep in thought, he developed a great love and respect for nature. This was expressed in his Sixth Symphony, the *Pastoral*, which describes the life of ordinary country folk.

A cornfield, painted by Peter de Wint. Beethoven had a great love of the countryside and affectionate respect for the people who worked it.

Napoleon's brother, Jérôme Bonaparte (1784–1860), was King of Westphalia from 1807 to 1813. He returned to French politics in 1847 when his nephew, Napoleon III, was on the throne.

The Congress of Vienna. Once Napoleon's power had crumbled, it was crucial for Europe's leaders to agree on a plan for the future.

Napoleon's army retreats from Moscow, 1812.

THE FALL OF NAPOLEON

Although a dictator, Napoleon proved himself to be a capable ruler. He made changes to the French system of law, the police, and education. He put strict controls on the Church and personally managed the army, which he relied on for his power. He introduced a new French aristocracy and put members of his family on the thrones of conquered states. He married a daughter of the Austrian emperor and made his son King of Rome. Napoleon was over ambitious, however. After a long war his army was defeated in Spain, and he lost nearly half a million troops while retreating through a bitter Russian winter following a failed attack on Moscow in 1812. His enemies united against him, and he was forced into exile on the island of Elba in 1814. Shortly afterward he managed to escape back to France, where he reformed his army. He was finally defeated at Waterloo and sent to St. Helena, an island in the South Atlantic, from which there was no escape. He died in 1821.

A NEW ORDER IN VIENNA

After more than twenty years of war in Europe, Napoleon eventually fell from power. His disastrous retreat from Russia in 1812 was followed by defeat at Waterloo in 1815, and exile, thousands of miles away, on the island of St. Helena. Peace was established. Vienna, which had suffered bombardments and invasions by the French, was now the center of peace talks. The **Congress of Vienna**, held from 1814 to 1815, drew Europe's leaders together, with the aim of stamping out revolutionary ideas, putting an end to the changes that were under way, and restoring the old order. One result was that the French royal family—the Bourbons—were returned to power.

This new settlement for Europe was masterminded by the Austrian statesman **Prince Clemens Metternich**. In Vienna, Metternich did everything he could to make his plan work: secret police, spies, and censorship were all used to silence anyone who agreed with the aims of the French Revolution.

The Viennese people were told to forget about politics and just enjoy themselves. Many parties and dances were held in the city, and people discovered the pleasures of country walks.

A good home life was also encouraged, particularly after the Emperor Francis I said that he thought the most important things in life were a strong family and a well-organized household.

This new interest in home life started a fashion in Viennese art. It concentrated more on small, delicate objects that would not only look pretty, but also be used in the homes of ordinary citizens. There were interesting new designs for clocks, glasses, coffeepots, chairs, and cabinets. The name that is often given to this period in art is **Biedermeier**.

Vienna had changed since Beethoven had first arrived in 1792. Then most works of art were enormous and impressive, because they were being done specially for the Emperor and a small group of very rich aristocrats.

Prince Clemens Metternich (1773–1859), who acted as political chairman of the Congress.

The Emperor of Austria, Francis I, arriving in Vienna, 1814. Metternich's steady influence helped Francis win the devotion of his people.

At Odds with the World

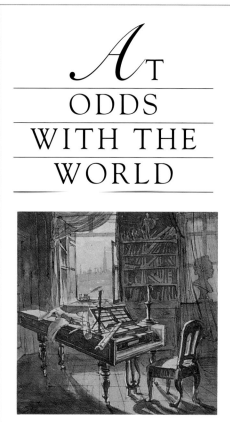

Beethoven's study. This drawing was done just three days after the composer's death.

 eethoven was not the right sort of person to fit into this new Viennese way of life. He hated parties, he had no wife or home, and his liberal beliefs were considered wicked. Everyone agreed he was the greatest composer alive, but his music was considered far too difficult and serious for the mood of Vienna at that time. People were also a little confused by his wild and disorganized appearance. So Beethoven locked himself away and kept silent.

After completing his seventh and eighth symphonies in 1812, Beethoven seems suddenly to have lost the will to compose much else. His fame was greater than ever, but for six years he wrote very little. His last attempt at playing the piano in public, in 1814, was a disaster. By 1818 his hearing had gone completely. If he wanted a conversation with someone, it had to be written down on paper. He became more and more peculiar, sulky, and suspicious of people. He would occasionally be seen, walking on his own, muttering to himself, as if in a daydream, and scribbling down little musical notes in a shabby sketchbook.

His life was also changed by the death of his brother Caspar in 1815. Beethoven was determined to bring up Caspar's nine-year-old son, Karl, as if he were his own. He fought long battles in court to keep the boy away from his mother, and could think of little else for several years. This is another reason why he composed so little at this time. In the end, it became like an obsession, and he even forgot to consider Karl's own happiness.

Uncle and nephew did not understand each other very well, and matters reached an ugly climax in 1826 when Karl attempted to shoot himself. Beethoven felt responsible and never really recovered from the shock. Karl eventually joined the army and lived until 1858.

Beethoven would often be seen walking the streets of Vienna, lost in thought. He sometimes forgot other people were there, even his nephew Karl.

FACE TO FACE WITH GOD

The composer's last years saw him complete three extraordinary projects: a full-scale church **mass**, his Ninth Symphony, and a set of extremely complicated string quartets. These final works are the result of a whole lifetime's musical pondering. They were written slowly, with every note carefully placed, so that the music would be completely true to Beethoven's vision. There is something religious, or sacred, about the way in which he approached these works. In fact, when one of the violinists complained that the last quartets contained music that was too difficult to play, Beethoven replied, "I can't think about your miserable violin when I'm speaking to my God!"

A violin used in the earliest performances of Beethoven's string quartets.

The mass, known as the *Missa Solemnis*, was dedicated to his old friend and patron the Archduke Rudolph, to celebrate his being made a **cardinal**. It took rather longer to complete than expected, and missed the cardinal's installation by three years!

The Ninth Symphony is exciting in many ways. It is Beethoven's longest symphony and takes over an hour to perform. It also includes a vast choir and solo voices in the last **movement**, which is why it is known as the *Choral* Symphony. The sung words are by the German poet Schiller and are entitled "Ode to Joy." Schiller, like Beethoven, believed in equality and freedom for all people. He was also considered a little too revolutionary for the political rulers of his time. Beethoven's musical setting of this joyous poem is a fitting tribute to both men's dream of a better world.

Archduke Rudolph, younger brother of the Emperor Francis I, in his robes as Cardinal of Olmütz.

According to one story, Beethoven stood rather sadly at the end of the first performance (1824), assuming the audience had not enjoyed his work. It was not until he was tapped on the shoulder that he turned around and saw what he could not hear: rapturous applause.

Right, an imaginary scene showing the composer Franz Liszt playing a tribute to the memory of Beethoven. The others paying their respects are (left to right) the writers Alexandre Dumas, Victor Hugo, and George Sand, and the composers Niccolò Paganini and Gioacchino Rossini.

Five string quartets, originally commissioned by prince Galitzin, were the last complete works by Beethoven. Soon after Karl's attempted suicide, he was confined to bed for three months, suffering from **dropsy** (brought on by a failure of the liver). During this time he entertained himself by studying the works of **Handel**, and was visited by a large number of admirers, including his young contemporary, the composer **Franz Schubert**.

At 5:45 P.M. on March 26, 1827, it is said there was a clap of thunder and a flash of lightning over Vienna. If legend is to be believed, Beethoven lifted his eyes to heaven and shook a fist, before falling back against his pillow, dead. Twenty thousand Viennese people came out to watch his funeral procession. They were bidding farewell to a man whose influence in music is still felt today.

Franz Schubert (1797–1828) would spend many evenings surrounded by his friends, making music and discussing ideas. Although he was young enough to be Beethoven's musical heir, Schubert only outlived him by one year.

A plaster cast mask of Beethoven's face, made shortly after his death. The hollow cheeks show how thin he had become during his final illness.

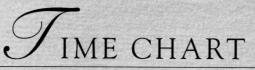

TIME CHART

1770	Ludwig van Beethoven born in Bonn, probably December 15.
1787	Beethoven visits Vienna and meets Mozart. Mother dies.
1789	French Revolution—storming of the Bastille, July 14.
1791	Mozart dies in Vienna, aged 36.
1792	French Republic proclaimed, and war with neighboring countries begins. Haydn passes through Bonn. Beethoven takes up residence in Vienna. Father dies.
1793	Louis XVI and Marie Antoinette executed in Paris.
1798	Beethoven completes *Pathétique* Sonata. First notices loss of hearing.
1802	Writes the Heiligenstadt Testament.
1803	Composes Third Symphony, *Eroica*.
1804	Napoleon crowns himself Emperor of France.
1805	Beethoven completes *Fidelio*. Napoleon occupies Vienna.
1806	Beethoven composes the Razumovsky string quartets.
1808	Completes the Fifth Symphony and composes the Sixth (*Pastoral*).
1809	Haydn dies. Beethoven agrees to remain in Vienna and accepts a salary for life. Napoleon bombards Vienna and invades again.
1812	Napoleon's retreat from Moscow.
1814	Third version of *Fidelio* performed. Congress of Vienna begins.
1815	Battle of Waterloo. Napoleon is exiled. Caspar van Beethoven dies, and his son, Karl, becomes the composer's ward (made legal, January 9, 1816).
1821	Napoleon dies on St. Helena.
1823	Beethoven completes the Mass in D (*Missa Solemnis*).
1824	Completes the Ninth Symphony (*Choral*).
1826	Karl van Beethoven attempts suicide. Last composition: String Quartet in F, op. 135.
1827	Beethoven dies in Vienna, March 26.

GLOSSARY

ambassador Someone who represents the interests of his or her own country in a foreign country.

aristocrat Someone who has inherited power, money, and property from his ancestors. An aristocrat usually has a title, such as duke, count, or earl. In the past an aristocrat often had a number of advisors and assistants who made up his court.

Bach, Johann Sebastian (1685–1750) A German composer who wrote many outstanding works for organ, harpsichord, church choir, and small orchestra.

Biedermeier The term used to describe the artistic movement that began in Vienna after the fall of Napoleon. Gottlieb Biedermaier (the spelling was changed later) was an invented character whose humorous poems were published in a weekly magazine.

Blake, William (1757–1827) An English poet, painter, and religious thinker. He often illustrated his own poems with powerful unconventional paintings, which showed his strong faith.

cardinal A very senior priest in the Roman Catholic Church. When the Pope, the head of the Church, dies, the cardinals have the responsibility of electing a new Pope.

Classical In musical terms this refers to the period from around 1750 to 1820. Compositions of this time generally followed certain formal structures, rather than allowing the composer to express his own feelings.

concerto A piece of music written for orchestra and solo instruments.

Congress of Vienna A meeting of Europe's leaders that took place in Vienna between 1814 and 1815, after the fall of Napoleon. It was an attempt to bring some order to Europe, following the great changes of the previous twenty years.

dialogue The spoken lines of a play or opera.

dictator A ruler who has absolute power over a country and will not allow himself to be removed from power by free elections.

dropsy A serious illness that causes fluids to build up in the body.

French Revolution Growing unrest in France led to the people of Paris storming the Bastille, a fortress prison, on July 14, 1789. In 1792 the monarchy was overthrown and a republic declared. The new republic was soon at war with much of the rest of Europe. The revolution suffered from food shortages and economic problems until Napoleon Bonaparte took power in 1799.

Friedrich, Caspar David (1774–1840) A German painter. Much of his work showed vast, awesome landscapes with human beings often included as small, insignificant figures.

Handel, George Frideric (1685–1759) A composer, born in Germany, who spent much of his working life in England. His most famous work is the *Messiah*.

harpsichord A keyboard instrument that was most popular from the beginning of the sixteenth century until the end of the eighteenth.

improvise To compose music while actually performing, rather than to play from memory or from written music.

Industrial Revolution A period of history roughly between 1750 and 1850. The machines and technology invented during this period led to factories being built across Europe.

Kapellmeister The chief musician at the court of a ruler or aristocrat. The name means "master of the chapel" as the Kapellmeister was originally in charge of the musicians of the royal chapel, or Kapelle. Later his responsibilities were extended to include all of the court musicians.

keyboard The part of a harpsichord, piano, organ, or similar musical instrument that the musician uses to produce the sounds. Each key produces a different note.

mass An important part of worship in the Catholic Church. Many composers have been inspired to set the mass to music.

Metternich, Prince Clemens (1773–1859) An Austrian statesman who brought European leaders together to fight Napoleon and who played an important part in the Congress of Vienna after Napoleon's defeat.

movement A piece of music that forms part of a larger composition. A typical symphony or concerto is divided into three or four movements.

Neefe, Christian Gottlob (1748–98) A German musician who was court organist to the Elector of Cologne. He had an important influence on Beethoven, teaching him the works of J. S. Bach.

opera A musical drama in which the performers sing most or all of their lines, usually accompanied by an orchestra. The music is just as important as the words in an opera.

oppression Cruelty and injustice used by a government as a means of keeping people under its control.

overture A piece of music for orchestra that is played before the action starts in an opera. A concert overture was a single movement work sometimes written as the opening piece for a concert.

patron Somebody who supports an artist by providing money or employment.

plectrum (plural: plectra) A small thin piece of horn, wood, or other material for plucking the strings of some musical instruments. The strings in a harpsichord are sounded by plectra when the keys are struck.

Purcell, Henry (1659–95) An English composer who wrote many works for singers and instrumentalists. He is considered to be one of England's finest composers.

quartet A piece of music written to be performed by four musicians. A quartet is also the name given to a group of four musicians.

republic A country that is governed by the people or on behalf of the people by others they have elected. A republic is not ruled by a king, queen, emperor, or other ruler who has simply inherited power.

Romantic A term used to describe some of the art, writing, and music of the late eighteenth and nineteenth centuries. The Romantics were fascinated by nature and placed great value on the worth of individual experience.

Schiller, Johann Christoph Friedrich von (1759–1805) German poet and playwright whose work championed the cause of political freedom.

Schubert, Franz (1797–1828) An Austrian composer whose finest works may perhaps be found in the more than 600 songs he wrote. In addition, he composed magnificent music for piano, for quartets and other small instrumental groups, and for orchestra. Schubert was one of the greatest composers who ever lived.

sonata A piece of music written for piano or for another instrument accompanied by piano. A sonata usually has three or four movements.

symphony A piece of music written for orchestra. A symphony usually has three or four movements.

tuberculosis A serious infection that attacks the lungs. Before a cure was found, tuberculosis killed many people.

virtuoso A particularly skillful performer who has mastered all the techniques of playing his or her chosen musical instrument.

Waldstein, Count Ferdinand von (1762–1823) An influential German aristocrat and amateur musician who encouraged Beethoven to compose as a young man.

Watt, James (1736–1819) A Scottish engineer whose experiments and discoveries led to the production of an efficient steam engine. Steam engines led to the rise of the factories and the Industrial Revolution.

Wordsworth, William (1770–1850) An English poet who wrote passionately about his feelings toward nature. As a young man he visited France and became a supporter of the French Revolution.

INDEX

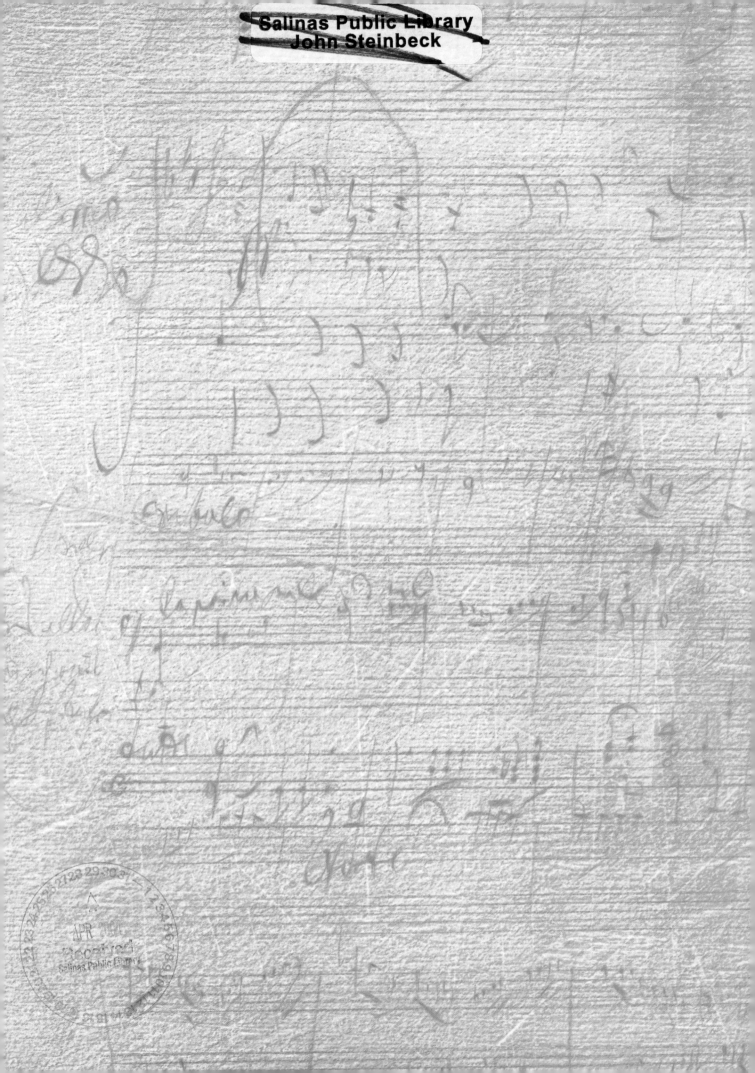